Wildlife in Derbyshire

by Jean Woolley

Photographs by Stuart Whitehead

CONTENTS

Published by Derbyshire Countryside Ltd.

Heritage House, Lodge Lane, Derby DE1 3HE

Telephone 01332 347087   Fax 01332 290688

Printed in Great Britain   ISBN 0 85100 126 2

A baby grey
squirrel

by keeping eyes
and ears open and
taking the time to
look around, you'll
rarely be
disappointed.

A grey wagtail

INTRODUCTION

This book is written purely as a celebration, in words and pictures, of the beauty and diversity of the countryside around us. All observations were gained first hand around the county and although I've had a lifelong interest in the countryside around me, I make no claim to be a wildlife expert.

The motivation behind the book was a desire to share my enthusiasm and experiences in a reader-friendly, easy-on-the-eye, leisurely ramble through the wilds of Derbyshire. You don't have to be an expert in natural history to delight in the splendid array of local flora and fauna. There is immense satisfaction to be had from going out and observing at first hand nature in all its guises, from the smallest beetle crawling over a leaf to the vast windswept emptiness of a heather-clad moor. I make no apologies for dwelling on some subjects more than others. Everyone has their favourite places or subjects that they return to time after time. There are few precise locations mentioned in the book stating that you'll find a particular bird here or a certain butterfly there, but the various habitats written about can all be found in Derbyshire. Discovering the places for yourself and becoming acquainted with their inhabitants is surely half the fun. The countryside and its wildlife will remain a constant source of discovery and enjoyment, that is freely available to everyone, provided the rules and codes of the countryside are adhered to. But it is worth considering these things from another viewpoint. Regardless of who owns the land, to the creatures that live there, it is their home and you are the visitors. They deserve the same courtesy and respect you would give to a neighbour or friend when visiting their home. Keep this in mind when you're out and about, because at the end of the day, 'if we abuse it, we lose it'.

There can't be anything more enjoyable than going for a walk in the countryside – the peacefulness of a country lane; a rarely trodden footpath that winds through fields and over hills; woods that have a cool greenness even on the hottest days, and all seemingly waiting to be charted for the first time. Round every corner and in every wood and field there's something new to be discovered. For me there isn't a better way to spend an hour or two and when time allows, a whole day. Weather conditions, even the time of day, can make a world of difference to the wildlife you might come across. Use field guides for some general information on what to look for, when and where. But by keeping eyes and ears open and taking the time to look around, you'll rarely be disappointed.

Jean Woolley

SILENT HUNTERS

Snow had fallen in the night. Not heavily but enough to withstand the weak rays of an afternoon sun in late January. The dull grey brown countryside to the north of Ashbourne had taken on a crisp clean geometric quality. The road I was on was bordered by a mixture of hawthorn hedges and wooden fences. Most of the small birds were staying within the confines of these spiky hedges. I could see them perched among the branches or hopping about on the ground beneath. The dark tangle of these branches must have offered some protection against the weather and kept them hidden from the watchful eyes of predators. The hedges were also providing shelter for small clumps of snowdrops growing on the grassy verges. I am always amazed by how these tiny, fragile-looking plants can push their way up through the hard cold earth and produce such delicate white flowers that delight the eyes on wintry days like this.

After another bend in the road I could see Ashbourne in the distance. Fifty yards on I carefully brought the car to a halt. About fifteen feet ahead of me perched on the fence was a little owl, its speckled feathers were fluffed up against the cold. His back was towards me but as I switched off the engine his head swivelled round. For a second or two, large yellow eyes stared in my direction, then he quickly took flight across the fields towards a small wood. The little owl is not a native of Britain. It was introduced to the Midlands from the Continent in the late nineteenth century and it quickly established itself throughout England and Wales.

The little owl is one of our three most familiar owls. The other two being the tawny and barn owls. Of these, it is the little owl that we are most likely to see during the day, bobbing in the grass or on a perch searching for food. I once saw one in a tree in the middle of a football ground car park. It was a busy match day with cars and people coming and going continuously. The owl was quite unperturbed. Sitting on a high branch leaning on the trunk it dozed in the afternoon sun. Though the most common and widespread, tawny owls are rarely seen during the day, these are the owls that send their eerie calls into the darkness. One lives in the woods behind my house and on many an autumn night keeps me awake with his hooting. Sadly barn owls are declining rapidly and it is a few years since I saw one of these superb silent hunters in the wild. I'd been visiting friends and was taking a short cut home through the fields. It was a warm evening and I'd stopped to watch the bats skimming overhead.

*The little owl often
seen in daylight*

4

The numerous and highly vocal tawny owl – Derbyshire's most frequently heard owl

The beautiful but endangered barn owl

Suddenly a pale ghost-like form flew across the grass towards me. I remember staring in open-mouthed wonder as the barn owl swerved away from me and disappeared over a hedge only yards from where I was sitting. As I drove on towards Ashbourne I hoped this encounter with a barn owl wasn't to be my last.

LIVING BERRIES

Mid-morning of an early spring day, the sun was bright in the sky. A few clouds raced across the wide expanse of blue, an indication of the strength of the bitingly cold wind. I'd heard in a roundabout way that snakes had been seen in this area of Heage. Not knowing this part of Derbyshire very well I wasn't sure whether I should be looking for signs of grass snake or adder. It could even have been a slow worm – a legless lizard often mistaken for a snake. That's if there were any to be seen here at all!

I took the road past Heage windmill. It stood tall and proud on the hilltop, the sails shining brilliant white in the sunlight. About a mile further on I parked the car in a layby and climbed the stile. A steady uphill walk through open fields soon warmed me up despite the chill wind. I reached Bessalone Wood that crowned the hill and looked around. There was no sign yet of new leaves appearing. The white bark of the trees gleamed in the sun, their branches standing out naked against the rich blue backdrop of the sky. Undergrowth was sparse, just a few gorse bushes. The yellow flowers were bright amongst the dark spiky leaves. Here and there the remains of last year's brambles trailed across the ground and clumps of dead bracken, brown and decaying, crumbled back into the earth. I couldn't imagine grass snakes living here, it was far too dry and sandy, vegetation would be scant even in summer. The outlying fields were well cultivated and cut too low to give cover to a wary snake. Adders, too, seemed unlikely inhabitants.

With a mental reminder to return later in the year, I walked down through the trees, climbed over a low dry-stone wall and onto the footpath that ran alongside the edge of the field. Gorse bushes grew in abundance beside the wall. Masses of golden blooms contrasted sharply with the grey stone and shadowy trees. I stepped nearer to the bushes. What had looked from a distance like clusters of small red berries among the flowers, on closer inspection, turned out to be ladybirds. They had emerged from winter hibernation and were catching the warmth of the sun before getting down to more important matters such as eating and breeding.

Left: Heage windmill

Right: Silver birch, the white bark gleaming in the sun

Below: Ladybirds emerge from their winter hibernation

COILS OF COLOUR

It was just over a week later and not much more than a mile away from the ladybirds, but things were totally different. The sun was shining brightly through thin clouds, the air was warm and a light breeze made scarcely a ripple on the waters of Cromford canal. An endless buzzing and chirping filled the air. Trees near and far shimmered with a hazy whisper of green. Hawthorn hedges had little rosettes of leaves sprouting from every branch. Reeds and other water plants had spear-like shoots reaching a good twelve inches out of the water, except for a small area near the far bank. In this area the reeds had been cropped short. It was the work of a water vole, who was nibbling at the base of the succulent green shoots; this is the most nutritious part of the plant. I stopped to watch the vole feeding, but ever wary of potential danger, it quickly disappeared with a plop beneath the water and swam to safety.

A water vole

This stretch of the canal isn't very deep and the bottom was easy to see. Staring into the still, clear water I spotted a small pike gliding stealthily through the reeds. Its brown grey colouring blended easily with the dappled colours in the water, making it difficult to see until it moved. A yard or two further along other small movements caught my eye. Male common toads were picking the best spots in the water to lie in wait for the females. After a few days of frenzied mating they would all go their separate ways till next year. Toads are solitary animals except at this time. They spend most of the day hidden away in their burrows or under logs. Warm rainy evenings and nights are the best time to look for them, when they're hunting for food.

On the opposite side of the canal from where I stood was a small field. It was bordered on two sides by a large wood that swept down to the water's edge. The wood looked to be quite old. Trees grew

After mating, common toads lead solitary lives.

randomly, not like the uniform rows you see in a managed plantation. Previous years' growth still covered the ground. Fallen trees and branches were left to lie, putting nutrients back into the soil. Those that had lain for a while had already been utilised by mosses and other creeping plants, their new spring growth beginning to hide the rotting bark.

The opposite bank of the canal dropped down steeply from the fenced field. It was dotted here and there with bushes and brambles, and the grass was already quite tall. The bank is only about a hundred yards long and ends abruptly near the wood. Here a huge rock sticks out of the bank, its base hidden in the reeds at the water's edge. Two or three shrubby trees grow close to it. The wood was peacefully inviting and I decided to go and explore. I crossed over the canal about half way along the bank via a narrow wooden plank. After only a few careful steps, I stopped and stared in amazement. Just a couple of yards ahead of

The fresh green foliage of spring adds a new dimension to the banks of the Cromford Canal at Ambergate

me was a grass snake, its head resting on the curves of its back. The olive green body gleamed in the sun, its yellow collar bordered with black, contrasting sharply. An occasional flicker of its long forked tongue was the only movement it made. An unconscious movement made by me had an immediate effect. Within seconds the snake, with a liquid flowing action, disappeared completely into the undergrowth. Searching the area where it had gone revealed nothing. Scanning the ground in front of me, I stepped as slowly and silently as

The common frog

9

possible, ears listening for the faint wooshing rustle that is often the only indication of a snake in the immediate vicinity – nothing. Next to the rock, I sat on a level bit of ground, got comfortable, and waited in the hope it might return.

A thin veil of cloud covered the sky now, so the sun cast no shadows, but it was still very warm. Ten minutes went by and just as I was considering carrying on to the wood, things started to happen. From somewhere beneath the rock, a pale browny-green head emerged. Tongue flicking rapidly in and out, it stopped, still partly hidden. The lithe body began to curve into an S-shape, with the head kept an inch or two off the ground, obviously alert to the slightest sign of danger. I guessed it to be about two foot long. At almost the same time another slid through the reeds directly beneath my feet. It left the water and glided gracefully towards the undergrowth at the base of the rock. Not daring to breathe for fear of being noticed, I watched fascinated as the sinuous body folded around itself in loose curves. The head was kept in the centre a little above the grass, tongue darting in and out tasting the air. This snake was also pale in colour, though more green than brown. Still glistening from its swim, the colours were rich and vibrant, making me wonder why people always seem more interested in exotic species when we have such beautiful ones right on our doorstep. Knowing that any sudden movements or strange noises would cause them to disappear, I rose cautiously, and managed to get a little closer to the snake by the rock. I could see the round black pupils rimmed with gold. Having no eyelids they always have the appearance of being wide awake.

Grass and brambles were beginning to encroach across the top of the rock though its exposed surface wasn't so bare. Grey green lichens had created mottled patterns on the flat top. A sudden shiver of excitement crept up my spine. There right on top of the rock

A grass snake basks in the spring sunshine; its head resting on the curves of its back

With its distinctive flowing action, the grass snake disappears into the undergrowth

in full view lay two more grass snakes. Both were dark green in colour, the yellow collars and black vertical stripes along their sides all looked clean and fresh. It could only mean that they had recently shed their skins after coming out of hibernation. The longer of the two must have been over three foot long and about two inches across at its thickest part. As I stood and watched, the clouds parted and the sun blazed bright. Reflected light off the water dazzled my eyes. I turned my head and took a sideways step, catching my foot in the trailing brambles. Only a small movement on my part but enough to send the snakes darting for cover. Though I saw exactly where they'd gone into the grass I could find no trace.

It was as if they had never been there. Looking at my watch I realised I'd spent nearly two hours with the grass snakes. My mind was still filled with wonderful images of these beautiful creatures when I became aware that it was raining. Exploration of the wood would have to wait. I retraced my steps back over the canal, noticing as I did, the changes that the rain was making to the scene. The canal was churned up to a murky brown colour, hiding anything that might be moving in it. Water was beginning to drip off every branch and twig as birds fluffed up their feathers to keep warm and dry. Sheep in a nearby field huddled together in one corner, their lambs pushing in among the crowded bodies to feed on their mothers' warm milk. Distant hills were now shrouded in mist and the fields took on a grey hue. The optimism of a spring morning had been washed away with the rain. No amount of rain could dampen the thrill of seeing those grass snakes in their natural habitat. Knowing snakes are in the area is no guarantee that any will be seen, as I was to discover on subsequent visits to the canal. Perhaps it's this uncertainty that is part of the attraction I have for them.

WHO'S WHO?

It doesn't matter whether you choose to follow one of the many designated footpaths in Derbyshire or wander along where fancy takes you, it's the plants and flowers that create the first impressions. With the flowers come the insects. Most noticeable are the butterflies and moths. At various times between spring and autumn caterpillars will also appear on their particular food plants. Some, but not all, are very difficult to detect. Ragwort, a common wayside plant was growing profusely along the verge of a well-used, wide footpath I was following. Feeding ravenously on its leaves were clusters of cinnabar moth caterpillars. These caterpillars feed almost exclusively on ragwort, taking in the plant's toxins. The bright yellow and black colouring of the caterpillar is a warning to birds and other predators that they are definitely not nice to eat. It was while watching them that I started thinking how few caterpillars bear any resemblance or give any indication as to what the adult moth or butterfly will look like.

The elephant hawkmoth caterpillar

There's the small, black, spiky larvae that become our well-known peacock butterflies. A rather flamboyant red, black and yellow caterpillar eventually emerges as a small mottled greyish-brown dagger moth. And how does a large, dark, clumsy–looking caterpillar like that of the elephant hawkmoth become transformed into the beautiful pink, mauve and gold night flyer? The colours and markings on moths and butterflies are often used in courtship, but I discovered that for some, scent plays an important role in finding a mate. I'd noticed on many occasions how some moths have large, feathery antennae. It's these that are used to pick up the airborne scent particles of a receptive mate, sometimes over great distances. Imagine being able to distinguish one particular scent from

A grey dagger moth caterpillar

among thousands, and be able to find the exact location of its source. In the middle of a town where alien human scents prevail, a moth like the feathered thorn would appear to have almost miraculous powers of discernment. What an amazing world we live in.

The striking yellow and black markings of the cinnabar moth caterpillar are a warning to predators

Feathered thorn moth

NATURE RECOVERED

When a large industrial site is cleared of all its buildings, rail tracks and machinery, the concrete, rubble and twisted pieces of metal that are left behind make a sad desolate picture. This was the scene when the ironworks side of a huge steel and concrete plant closed down. Luckily, the land, which is very close to where I live, is still owned by the steel company. It has never been redeveloped since its closure twenty years or so ago. Bordered on one side by a once busy canal and on the other by a meandering stream, this industrial scar has become a wildlife haven equal to many planned nature reserves. Spring and summer revel in a

Bank voles easily adapt to a change in environment

splendid show of wild flowers. The bright yellow of loosestrife and stonecrop, the pale pink of the delicate dog rose and the cheerful bobbing heads of oxeye daisies are just a few of the many species I've recognised while out walking. Old railway sleepers, contorted strips of metal and the odd-shaped pieces of broken concrete are all disappearing under a vast array of plants and shrubs, trees and grasses. A large reed bed near the perimeter of the site adds further to the diversity of habitat available for wildlife.

Rabbits, foxes and bank voles, grass snakes and lizards are all there. Birds, from small warblers and finches to woodpeckers and the stately heron are residents or regular visitors to the area. Apart from the endless bird song, the most dominant sound on a summer's day is the chirruping of grasshoppers. These little creatures can be seen springing about in the grass at your feet. As spring gets into its stride, insects and beetles of all shapes and sizes, emerge from their winter hibernation. The abundance and variety of plants and flowers attract them in great numbers. Most noticeable are the butterflies and moths. A leisurely stroll on a May morning, the sun bright and warm in the sky, can be rewarded with a wonderful display of colour. Flashes of orange or blue wings compete with bees for the best flowers. Reds, browns and yellows circle and dance in the air then settle tantalizingly close, only to take flight again, the second you move nearer. I love this time of

The delicate pale pink dog rose

year everywhere there's an air of expectancy – spring becomes an almost tangible experience. You can breathe it deep into your lungs, taste its freshness in the early morning breeze and hear the excited buzz of new life generating all around.

A viviparous or common lizard finds a sunspot amongst discarded concrete

Nutbrook stream
Main picture: a field of oxeye daisies

15

REFLECTIONS

Deciding not to carry on along the Nutbrook Canal I crossed the small wooden bridge. It spanned a narrow channel that connected the canal to a fair-sized lake used by anglers. With the fishing season over and few walkers about on this cold spring morning the lake area and surrounding wood were deserted. A footpath, only wide enough for one person, meandered round the edge of the lake, branching off at intervals through the trees. It was one of these branching pathways that I followed.

The few flowers that bloomed under the trees were taking advantage of the spring sunshine that filtered through the still sparse leafy canopy. Violets, growing in small clumps, peeped out from beneath low-growing shrubs and brambles. The odd bluebell and wild daffodil added a splash of colour.

I came to a fork in the path and took the one that gradually curved back towards the lake. Through a gap in the trees and bushes I could see the water. A pair of grebes were beginning their courtship. Sunlight twinkled and flashed off the gentle ripples created as they slid through the water. Round the edges the reeds were growing fast. They were already about a foot high. It was at this moment that I spotted a heron on the far side of the lake wading in the shallows. As I stood and watched he took three slow, deliberate steps further into the water and then became motionless. The neck was curved into an S-shape as the head was lowered towards the water, the long dagger-shaped beak pointing down only inches from the surface. I couldn't decide whether the yellow eyes, staring so intently, were looking for a fish dinner or admiring his sleek grey reflection. I took two or three more steps along the path. With his keen eyesight he was immediately aware of me even though I thought the trees and bushes were keeping me hidden. Forgetting his watery meal the heron raised his head and stared across at me. The breeze ruffled the feathers along his back and lifted the black plume on his head, but for the moment he made no other movement. With only about ten yards between me and the water's edge I decided to try and get even closer for a better view. My steps were as slow and deliberate as the heron's had been. Trying to stay screened by the bushes I managed to cover half the distance, but herons are extremely cautious birds and this one was no exception. He launched himself into the air and with slow, heavy

A heron perches at the top of a tree

Great crested grebes

wingbeats steadily circled the lake, before disappearing over the treetops. For all their caution and distrust of humans some herons will quite happily exploit us. I've heard many a tale of garden ponds being emptied of their fish stocks and some of our taller buildings being used as nest sites. It is more usual to see their large rough-looking nests made of small branches and twigs, grouped together in treetops.

STARS IN THE GRASS

Living on the outskirts of Ilkeston means that within thirty minutes of walking I can reach an assortment of wildlife habitats. Wooded areas containing both deciduous and coniferous trees, ponds and canals and open meadows. Rather surprisingly, some might think, the two places where I find the greatest variety of wildlife, in what are relatively small areas, have only recently become havens for a large number of birds, animals and insects. By recently I mean in the last twenty years or so. One is a disused railway cutting, the other, a once flourishing iron works.

The tracks of the railway line near Stanley village were removed many years ago, leaving a narrow pathway that is used frequently by people as a short cut to nearby villages.

A great tit

A chaffinch

Ramblers also make it part of their walks. The sloping banks are now overgrown with various kinds of bushes and trees. Nettles and tall grasses hide an assortment of wild flowers during the summer. The bridges are all that are left along this line and the trees that grow close to them give these places a gloomy appearance on dull overcast days. Walks I've taken along this track have revealed an array of wildlife. Finches can be seen flitting from bush to bush, bluetits and great tits, their colours flashing in the sunlight, dart through the trees. And if you are able to recognise their different sounds, blackbirds, thrushes and warblers, to name just a few, all contribute to the bustling symphony of life on the wing. Even the often heard but seldom seen cuckoo has been spotted criss-crossing the treetops

Male blackbird

A little owl

on a warm June evening. I was lucky enough on one occasion to see a little owl rise up from the grass in front of me and disappear into leafy branches not far ahead. Small animals I've rarely seen, except for bats silently winging their way up and down the cutting, catching moths and other night-flying insects. Butterflies, moths, bees and a considerable assortment of other insects and beetles can be detected, though some not as welcome as others. I'm not sure whether it's the arrival of a human being or just a hot summer's afternoon, maybe a mixture of both, that brings out all the biting insects. Midges, gnats

A song thrush

and the like seem to have a radar system especially for locating people. There are days when a suit of armour might be the best defence against them. Despite this I will return year after year for one outstanding spectacle, glow-worms!

A painted lady butterfly feeding on a thistle

My first encounter with these remarkable beetles, for that's what they are, was many years ago. I was about eight and my family were holidaying in Cornwall. Though only about thirty years ago, people were less guarded about letting their children wander unsupervised. My parents were no exception. It was late evening and, as usual, I'd been exploring the open countryside near to where we were staying. Leaning on a fence staring up at the dark velvety blue sky, I watched the stars slowly appear. Shimmering faintly at first, they blazed radiantly, like small silver fires in the night sky. My eyes started to water from staring so hard, I rubbed them and lowered my gaze to the ground. What I saw made me catch my breath. It seemed the stars had fallen into the grass. Was I imagining things? I rubbed my eyes again in disbelief! The points of light were still there, green and glowing. A sense of wonder came over me. Never before had I seen or heard of anything like this. It was like standing in the middle of a fairytale and I tingled inside. Heart pounding anxiously, I knelt in the grass and gently eased one of the tiny neon lights into the palm of my hand. The female glow-worm, as I later discovered it to be, was slightly over half-an-inch long. The body was made up of overlapping segments with a head that reminded me of a battle helmet. But it was no armour plating I felt, just a velvety softness. The last three segments of the insect's body that had previously been a bright luminous glow slowly dimmed, so I carefully placed it back in the grass with the other female glow-worms. Soon her light would be glowing bright again in the quest to attract a male. Standing up I took another look around me. The points of light were still shining and I wouldn't have been surprised to see tiny figures dancing between the grass stars. Reluctantly I made my way back to our holiday home. I had no opportunity to see them again as we left the next day.

It wasn't until I was married with children of my own that I returned to Cornwall to look for the glow-worms. An extensive search revealed nothing, so I made enquiries at the local nature conservancy council, only to be told that the colony had died out many years before due to insecticide spraying.

To hear by word of mouth that glow-worms existed almost on my doorstep didn't raise much enthusiasm in me as information gained in this way can be very unreliable. Still, it was worth an investigation, if only to discover what other wildlife was there. That's how I found the railway cutting a couple of years ago. I visited the place a few times during the day to get to know the area before making a night-time search for the glow-worms.

A warm evening late in June found me sitting on a log watching the stars appear in the sky just as I had those many years before. As darkness closed in I switched on my torch and stepped onto the narrow path. I walked slowly to avoid stumbling into the tall nettles that grew on either side of me on this part of the path. The beam of light illuminated the path for only a yard or two ahead of me. Minutes passed and I began to feel despondent, the information I'd been given was starting to look as unreliable as I'd come to expect from such sources. The night was warm and peaceful and I was enjoying watching the bats skimming close over my head in their hunt for food. It wouldn't hurt to stay a while longer, so I turned to make my way back to the fallen log. Oh boy! I could see the lights. Heartbeat speeded up, the skin on the back of my neck prickled and I could feel myself shaking excitedly. After all these years the sensation of being in that other fairytale world had not left me. I stood transfixed as more of the tiny green beacons appeared before me. Time passed unheeded as I watched and examined these extraordinary creatures, but eventually I decided to make my way home. The streets were empty as I drove along except for a young fox caught in the beam of the headlights. He stopped and stared for a second, then quickly slipped through a gap in a nearby hedge. The rest of the world slept, I'd be joining them soon.

It seemed the stars had fallen into the grass.

A female glow-worm shining bright in her quest to find a mate

CURIOUS COWS

Reaching the stile at the end of the farm track I turned and looked back. The path was steep and almost straight, just a slight wiggle about half way up where it passed the farmhouse and outbuildings. White and dusty it ran between grey stone walls. The lower part, where it turned off from the main road, was partially hidden by trees, cool and shady. I hadn't been prepared for the sudden heat and dazzling glare as I emerged from beneath them. From over the wall came the lazy mooing of half-a-dozen beef cattle. Idly chewing at the lush green grass, only their tails swished tirelessly in a vain attempt to rid themselves of the clouds of irritating flies. The weather was unbelievably warm for late spring, but knowing how fickle the British weather is, I wasn't convinced for a moment that this was a foretaste of the summer to come. The track came to a halt at a wide metal gate adjoining the stone stile. It was the gate I was leaning on now as I looked back down the chalky stone path. Behind me to the north was an area known as Longway Bank, a mile to the south was the picturesque village of Alderwasley. Lifting my gaze to the horizon I was amazed by how high up I was. Green fields gave way to slate grey and red rooftops. Roads and lanes criss-crossed through towns and villages, dark woods and flourishing pasture. A hazy mist shimmering in the sun enveloped the distant hills, making it difficult to tell where earth and sky met.

Hawthorn,
may blossom

Squeezing through the narrow stile I followed the footpath that ran beside a tall hawthorn hedge. The heady sweet smell of its white flowers filled my nostrils. It almost masked the distinctive odour of cow dung, but not quite. The may-blossom completely covered the hedges and bushes, leaving little of their green leaves to be seen. Bees were feverishly employed collecting the nectar. They buzzed furiously at one another when they landed on the same flower, as if there wasn't enough to go round.

The footpath branched in many directions through the field, meandering over and around the many humps and hollows that are characteristic of many parts of Derbyshire. Turning off the main path I made my way up a rather steep hillock. The short springy grass was absent from parts of this and other slopes, revealing a loose, light, sandy soil. Gorse and bracken dominated many of the slopes.

The few low growing brambles that grew among them were sending out long trailers that would soon be snatching at and tripping up any unwary walker. The yellow gorse that is one of the earlier flowers to appear was already beginning to turn brown and look tatty, though a few bees were still searching among them. Taking the last few steps to the top of the hill I came to a sudden halt. Not ten yards away, coming up the other side, was a dozen young bullocks. I don't know who was more surprised, them or me. Noses thrust forward, they sniffed and snuffled inquisitively, all the while taking tentative steps towards me. After a minute or two I began walking towards them, shooing them off the path as I got closer. They trotted a few yards away, stumbling and sliding down the side of the hill in alarm. On the far side of the slope the drop was less steep and the track dipped gently down and disappeared round the bottom of the next hill.

Halfway down the slope something made me look back. The bullocks had overcome their initial fear and in a ragged line were following me like the rats followed the Pied Piper, at a safe distance of course. As I moved, they moved. When I stopped they stopped, the ones at the back craning their necks to see what the hold-up was. To anyone watching it must have looked a ridiculous sight. In a bizarre way these domesticated farm animals had turned the tables on me and I was being intensely scrutinised by them in the way I might study a creature in the wild. The thought of it made me laugh which probably appeared even more absurd. No amount of shooing, hand clapping or arm waving seemed to quell their curiosity. Making my way to the wall that bordered the far side of the field, I followed the track that ran beside it, until it reached the corner. There a wooden stile finally halted the bullocks' curiosity. They gazed forlornly after me as I climbed over the stile and carried on down the track. After about ten yards I looked behind me, tails swishing the bullocks were ambling their way back up the field to resume their grazing.

The path was wide, probably used for farm vehicles, bordered on one side by a stone wall and wooded area, on the other by a fence and open fields. Leaning on the fence I gazed down across the fields towards a large farmhouse and imposing white-fronted residence that nestled under the eaves of a wood that covered the far slope. A chilliness had crept into the wind - it was time to move on. Turning, I froze in mid-step. Ten yards away, perched on fallen logs, was a jay, our most exotic-coloured member of the crow family. For perhaps a second, we stared at each other, then this reticent bird was winging its way through the trees.

A jay, the most flamboyant member of the crow family

I marvelled at the colours. It's only when in full flight that the vivid, azure blue flashes on its wings are revealed enough to be fully appreciated. Blackbirds criss-crossed the lower branches in the wood, their warning staccato cries echoing across the fields. Watching them I noticed that they rarely flew upwards from trees, walls or fences. Blackbirds always seem to swoop down low across the ground before rising in normal flight. Rooks in the tree tops were having raucous slanging matches, wings flapping as they danced in excitement. Mosses and lichens covered the wall that bordered the wood, it looked and smelled old. If the rocks could speak they would surely have many a tale to tell. In many places the wall had crumbled and the grey stones were scattered on the ground. Ivy enveloped the remains, but I couldn't decide whether it was trying to hold the wall up or push more of it down.

Rounding a slight bend, the path sloped down towards another gate and stile. The fields and woods gave way to houses and factories. Tall chimneys and grey metallic constructions loomed over the tree tops, and a large expanse of dark fir-wood looked to be marching over the horizon. Gathering grey clouds furnished a sombre backdrop to the scene.

Dropping my gaze to the nearer pathway I surveyed the assortment of bracken and bushes that was dotted along the side of the stone wall. A splash of bright colour caught my eye. Something, I wasn't sure what, at this distance, was gleaming pink in a shaft of sunlight. It was partly hidden by the bushes and the occasional gusts of wind kept pushing it out of sight. Reaching the bushes I discovered a beautiful foxglove, standing majestically amidst the green and grey. A solitary furry bumble bee was methodically visiting each bell-like flower. The insides of these coral pink caves are speckled with black dots surrounded by white. In the wild I've never seen foxgloves grow in large groups, but with their imposing stature and brilliant colouring a single plant will attract insects (and people) wherever they are found growing. As I studied the flowers another bee joined the first and there was quite a bit of excited buzzing as they both tried to get into the same flower. Leaving the bees to their tireless work I carried on to the lower gate. Here the path divided. One path led down past the farmhouse, the other curved round behind the wood, disappearing over another steep rise. Which path to take was decided for me by the weather. The gathering grey clouds picked this moment to release their abundant supply of rain. I retraced my steps but kept to the lower paths. The hills I'd walked up earlier were becoming slippery, it wouldn't have been much fun sliding to the bottom on my back. The bullocks were nowhere to be seen but their occasional throaty moos could be heard in the distance.

Despite the rain, birds continued their singing. A mixed chorus of warbles, chirps and twitters echoed over the fields from trees and bushes. The clamorous diatribe of crows and rooks rang out at intervals above the melodious birdsong, shattering the peaceful though wet scene. Clouds and rain seemed to drain the colours from around me. It's almost as if the sombre greyness gets inside you making you feel as gloomy as your surroundings. As I reached the white path the sun broke through a gap in the clouds. It was a signal for activity to start again. Birds left the shelter of the hedgerows and trees and as I walked down the white stony lane, now turned to a milky sludge, they darted here and there in buoyant excitement at the sun's heartening light and warmth.

A beautiful foxglove, standing majestically

Chaffinch

Mining Bee on a water mint

The restful green
of the wood

TRACKS THROUGH THE TREES

It would be difficult to choose a favourite time of day for walking. There are memorable encounters to be had at any hour. Like the day I was standing at the edge of Crich Chase near Ambergate, looking up across a grassy field, waiting for the sun to appear above a tall hawthorn hedge. An early morning mist covered the low hill in a translucent veil, blurring the outlines of trees and bushes. Birds had been up and about for some time, their whistles and chirps ringing out over the fields. I could hear them winging through the branches of the wood behind me. It was late spring when they'd be at their busiest, feeding growing families.

The remains of a fallen tree provided me with a dry seat, the grass was still wet from the early mist and dew. Relaxed, I took in the dreamy atmosphere of my surroundings. My first sight of the sun was through a blue haze, it looked cold and gave little heat at this hour. As the minutes passed the blue mist took on a golden hue, the sun burned stronger and everything became clear, the colours fresh and vivid. The appearance of the sun was like a cue for daily life to begin in earnest. Bees, from the large hairy bumble bee, moving ponderously from flower to flower, to the small drones zipping here and there, trying to collect as much nectar as possible in the shortest time. The birds became more active, passing to and fro over the fields in front of me. Two or three swallows skimmed across the top of the grass then wheeled up into the sky feeding on the small insects that danced and darted in the sunshine. A few butterflies vied with the bees for nectar. At first glance they were just dull brown creatures, hardly worth a second look. That was until one settled on a

The Comma butterfly's 'filigree pattern of black, orange and brown'

nearby flower. It slowly opened its wings and displayed a filigree pattern of black, orange and brown that seemed to glint in the sunlight. It made me realise that it is wrong to dismiss even the dullest looking creature. Closer examination might just reveal something unexpectedly beautiful. Getting to my feet I walked to the path through the trees. The sun cast long shadows across the ground in front of me. The new grass took on a rich hue in the early morning sunlight. Dew sparkled and flashed like diamonds, as blade and leaf quivered in the breeze. Of the few flowers that grow in wooded areas bluebells must be the most memorable and spectacular. Those great expanses of blue, viewed from a distance through misty sunlit trees, take on a surreal quality. Few of us appreciate how many

27

thousands of these tiny flowers it takes to produce such a scene.

For such a large wood there seemed to be no paths other than the main track through its centre. So, with eyes scanning the ground in front of me, I made my way through the thick tangle of undergrowth. In some places my feet sank deep into the leaf litter. It collected in drifts, hiding dips and hollows, tree roots and brambles and progress was cautiously slow in parts.

With bluebells being the most dominant flower, others often go unnoticed, either because the flowers are tiny and unobtrusive or they grow singly and don't have the same impact. Ramsons are one of the exceptions. They grow in the shadier places, the small white flowers, like six-pointed stars, sprout in clusters from a single tall stalk. They seem to float above the carpet of their rich green leaves.

Except for birdsong and the sound of flapping wings in the canopy above, the wood had a silent, empty feel about it. There was little evidence of other animals, except for rabbit droppings on the higher more open slopes. I looked up through the thinning trees to the top of the steep hill. Huge outcrops of limestone rock dominated the skyline. Though small compared with the towering cliffs in other parts of the county, I was still filled with a sense of awe at the great antiquity and enduring strength that was impressed upon me by them. Scrambling over and around half buried boulders and rocks I made my way down through the trees to more level ground.

What appeared to be a miniature pathway ran through the grass in front of me. Curiosity prompted me to take a closer look. As the grass had not been worn away entirely there was no likelihood of seeing any identifiable footprints. I followed it for a number of yards till it entered a small clearing. Glancing down at my feet to avoid tripping over a fallen branch, it became clear how and why the path had been formed. A steady procession of brown wood ants marched purposefully along the track in the opposite direction to me. My shoes were investigated by the workers as they passed by. Taking a sideways step off the path

A wood ants' nest

I watched as the flow of ants increased in number, giving me the impression of a brown rippling stream. I knew the nest site wouldn't be far away and carried on across the clearing. At the far side, screened by brambles and small bushes, stood the ants' home. It was a huge mound, at least two foot high, made of leaves, twigs and wood chips. The heap seethed and bubbled with thousands of these tiny insects, and thousands more were making their way along the trail. The ant colonies in my back garden were miniscule by comparison. Leaving the ants to their foraging I carried on down the slope through the trees. The sun was almost overhead. Its light was gently diffused as it filtered through the fresh green of the leaves above me. It is said that green is a very restful colour. Walking amongst the trees and undergrowth, yellow and green light flickering all around me, I wholeheartedly agreed.

FLYING FREE

It was the shape of the wings that made me stop and take a second look. They were long and pointed, with a backward sweeping curve. It was definitely a falcon but squinting into the bright May morning sky the gleaming white clouds blurred its outline, making it difficult to identify. I quickly picked up my binoculars and adjusted them. For several minutes I followed the bird's aerial dance, soaring and gliding in leisurely circles above Twyford. It was only as it passed overhead and disappeared behind a thick belt of trees that it flew low enough for me to recognise. It was a peregrine falcon. I could even see the characteristic black moustache. I let out a loud exclamation of surprise. They are an extremely rare sight in the Midlands and I felt a surge of pleasure inside me as the realisation dawned that I'd actually seen a peregrine flying wild and free in the sky above me. These are birds that breed on sea cliffs and the high crags of upland Britain. What was it doing here in Southern Derbyshire without a cliff in sight? My question was answered about a week later. Driving by Willington Power Station I saw a notice on the gate. It read: *Peregrine Watch Car Park*. Telephone calls and enquiries ensued over the next few days. I discovered that back in the early 1990s three peregrine falcons had been spotted flying in the area and roosting on the enormous cooling towers. Looking at the tall almost vertical sides of the towers I saw what a good substitute for cliffs they were. From the top they gave a wide view of the surrounding countryside while affording a fairly secure nesting site. In the hope of encouraging them to breed, a small platform was affixed to the access doorway near the top of number two tower. Over subsequent years a number of chicks have been successfully reared by the peregrines.

These graceful birds, often described as the ultimate flying machine because of their acrobatic skills, feed almost exclusively on pigeons and gulls, killing their prey in mid-air after a breathtaking power-dive. It is this preference for pigeons that brought about an unusual but official government policy during the Second World War. Fearing that this quite large falcon would kill the homing pigeons carrying vital messages they were ordered to be killed on sight. Persecuted over the last two centuries by gamekeepers, destroyed in large numbers during the last war and falling foul of unscrupulous nest robbers, I wasn't surprised to learn that there are probably fewer than a thousand breeding pairs in Britain today.

A sunny afternoon in June found me leaning on a fence staring across the fields towards the power station. It seemed strangely ironic that this monumental structure of bustling industry should be home to a creature we associate with high cliffs and remote wild places.

*The peregrine falcon,
moustached master of
the air at home at
Willington power station*

LEAVING HOME

The walk had been enjoyable, first along Cromford canal and then up onto the gentle slopes at the edge of Crich Chase. Now I was sitting on a flat grey rock that was half buried in the ground. Below me Ambergate lazed in an afternoon sunshine that gave the grass and leaves around me a yellow hue. May blossom had disappeared from the hawthorn but now clusters of small white flowers were beginning to appear on the elder bushes. Many birds were criss-crossing between the bushes and hedges. Mostly sparrows and bluetits, but I recognised some finches and a small band of long-tailed tits. Some of these birds were clearly feeding hungry families. For a few minutes I sat there listening to the different bird calls and trying to match them to their owners. My attention was suddenly drawn towards a tangle of bushes about ten yards to my left. On one of the lower branches sat a young bluetit. I had the feeling he'd only just ventured out of the nest. The last remnants of fluffy down were still sticking out from among the adult feathers and there was a trace of yellow edging round his beak. Occasionally a parent bird came with food for the fledgling. I watched how he gestured frantically each time an adult came near. With head

A young bluetit waits patiently for its next meal

tucked in and half opened wings fluttering steadily, a plaintive but insistent stream of chirps came from a gaping mouth. Very soon he would have to fend entirely for himself.

So engrossed was I with the actions of the bluetits that I didn't at first notice the unfamiliar sounds filtering in among the surrounding birdsong. It reminded me of the staccato alarm call of a blackbird, but slower deeper and in shorter bursts. It was coming from the narrow strip of woodland behind me. Curiosity sent me walking towards the trees trying to pinpoint the exact location from where the noise was coming.

Still some yards away from the trees I noticed a great spotted woodpecker as it flew out from among the branches. I felt certain this beautiful black and white bird was connected with the mystery noise. Reaching the edge of the wood I stopped and turned, waiting to see if the woodpecker would return. Now I was closer I realised there was more than one bird making the strange

Swallows and house martins talk on the telephone wires

sound. I guessed at least three. The calls suddenly became louder and more excited. I looked around and was just in time to catch sight of the woodpecker as it came back over the fields towards the trees. It had an unusual undulating flight that made it look as if it were bouncing along on a current of air. Without slowing it entered the trees. I followed quickly, though this wasn't as easy as it had first appeared. A tumbledown dry-stone wall bordered the wood. The stones had been elbowed out of place over the years by the expanding trunks and roots. Trailing brambles looked as if they were trying to hold onto them and stop them rolling down the hill. It seemed to be working. I scrambled and teetered over the stones, grumbling under my breath at the needle sharp, grasping bramble thorns. There was little or no pathway under the trees and the thick undergrowth hid the uneven ground. Luckily I didn't have to go far, after about ten yards the clamorous chirps were right above me. Though I stared up into the branches till my neck ached all I could see were shadowy forms moving through the profusion of dappled green leaves. Even the adult woodpecker, whom I hoped was the parent bird, had disappeared again. I started to move around the small group of trees that the hidden birds were occupying, still peering up at the tall trunks. Then I spotted it, just where the main trunk of the tree started to branch off. A neat round hole caught in a shaft of sunlight. Framed in the hole was the head of a great spotted woodpecker, the last one in the nest. The juvenile red cap was clearly visible. This and the wispy bits of down on its head gave it a manic punk-like appearance. The parent bird did return and continued to do so at intervals, to bring food, but only it seemed for the one in the nest. No amount of excited calling from the other fledglings made any difference. The adult always landed on the one tree and with a hopping walk made its way to the nest hole where the greedy youngster waited with strident calls and gaping mouth. As the late sun dropped towards the horizon the vociferous woodpeckers gradually became quiet. Returning the next morning I found the nest empty and the wood silent to their calls. Hopefully the hole would be used again in the years to come.

A young great spotted woodpecker is still unsure about leaving the safety of its nest hole

Long-tailed tit

MAGIC STORMS

Standing at my back door I gazed languidly up at the sky. The afternoon was becoming more oppressive by the minute. Thick and heavy, the gathering grey clouds took on a faint brownish hue as they heaved and folded in on themselves. As the hot stifling air drained the energy from everything around, a hushed stillness settled about the place. Leaves on the bushes and trees hung limp. Birds stopped their whistles and chirps and the buzz and hum of insects became noticeably absent. Along with everything else I unconsciously held my breath and waited.

A faint faraway rumble reverberated across the sky. Seconds later the clouds released their torrent of water. Lightning flashed and crackled in all directions and the thunder rumbled and crashed almost without pause. A warm gusting wind brought the trees back to life, bending their branches to and fro in an exciting dance. The vast uncontrollable power of a thunderstorm has always held a fascination for me and I stood watching intently. My gaze was drawn from the fantastic spectacle above to small movements in the grass around me. Frogs, not running to find shelter as most other creatures were doing, but seemingly taking a leisurely stroll in the 'good' weather. What is it about thunderstorms that affects frogs in this way that an ordinary downpour doesn't. The common frog is anything but common to look at. Their colours are as varied as the leaves of autumn. Pale greens and yellows, mottled browns and hints of russet. A close-up of a frog's eye resembles a man's signet ring, a stone of black jet set in a circle of gold filigree. Don't we always copy nature's best designs. As the storm overhead subsided and the grumbles of thunder grew more faint, birdsong again filled the air. The clouds broke and shafts of sunlight filtered through to the distant trees, creating islands of bright colours amongst the dull misty greens. A blackbird, looking wet and bedraggled, alighted on the grass some ten yards away from me. It stood for a minute fluffing up its feathers and preening its wings. After a final shake and a quick flap it proceeded to quarter the ground searching for spiders, beetles and worms that the rain had washed up. By now the sky was back to a clear blue with just the occasional cloud drifting slowly towards the horizon. Nature had had a washing day. The dry, dusty leaves and flowers sparkled and glistened anew and a fresh earthy smell filled the air.

A common frog

SUMMER SOUNDS

It was a perfect summer day, one that you only read about in story books. The sky was blue, but not just any blue, it was that smooth, ice-creamy sort of blue decorated with spoonfuls of vanilla white clouds. A hazy yellow mist shimmered on the far horizon. Numerous shades of green covered the landscape, from the dark almost black tones of a distant fir-wood and the brilliant emerald green of hawthorn to the pale yellow-green of hay fields. The variety seemed endless. Dotted here and there were fields of rape. The bright iridescent yellow flowers dazzled the eyes making it difficult to focus on other things for a minute or two. I was sitting on a grassy bank a short distance from the busy A38 near Heage, gazing out across the lush-looking farmland. Cows grazed some of the fields, but the majority were given over to an assortment of crops. Continuing fine weather had prompted the farmers to commence the hay cutting. Two fields near me already had the grass lying in flat rows, drying in the sun.

The occasional hum of a car passing by on the road behind me blended in with the buzzing and whirring of nearby insects, strangely adding to the peacefulness. From behind the nearest farmhouse and buildings came the sound of a tractor being started up. It turned into a neighbouring field and soon that too started to look like a striped green quilt. A light refreshing breeze blew across the fields towards me, bringing with it one of summer's most enjoyable smells – new mown hay. It's a warm comforting smell that conjures up images of

The male kestrel - a view to a kill!

carefree childhood days when mystery
wonder were always just around the corr
waiting to be found. Leaning bac
savouring the moment, I gazed, eyes ha
closed, at the assortment of birds that
wheeled and criss-crossed low over
the trees and fields in front of me.
Crows or rooks (how can you tell at a
distance) lifted themselves out of the

A collared dove

grass and flew with laughing cackles into nearby trees. Wood pigeons and collared doves
with their hypnotic cooing, making the day feel even lazier, passed over in small groups.
Odd ones settled on high posts or amongst tree branches, their calls carrying far over the
countryside. As the tractor chugged slowly round the field, I noticed a different bird, sleek
and brown and about the size of a pigeon. It hovered almost motionless about a hundred
feet above the ground. It was a kestrel, scanning the new-mown grass for mice and voles
that had been disturbed by the tractor's cutting blades. With barely a flick of its wings it
began to circle effortlessly in the sky overhead, taking it even higher. It then began to hover
again and, using binoculars, I took a closer look. The bright chestnut wings and blue-grey
colour on the head and tail showed it to be a male kestrel. Spread wide, the wings kept up
a continual fluttering and the all important tail tilted this way and that, keeping this
delightful falcon perfectly poised in mid-air. All the while, with head lowered, it searched
the ground for its prey. Lowering my binoculars to take in the whole scene, I watched as
the kestrel circled again then hovered over the adjoining field. Seconds passed, then in the
blink of an eye, the wings were folded and it plunged head first at breakneck speed towards
the grass. A hawthorn hedge hid the last few feet of its breathtaking dive, but almost
immediately, this master of the skies was airborne again, carrying its unfortunate prey in its

talons. I watched as it made its way to a
small copse. Whether it was to feed itself
or a growing family I'll never know. My
watch told me it was time to be heading
home so with great reluctance at having
to forsake the pervading sense of
timeless nostalgia, I got to my feet. A
small red damsel-fly buzzed past my
head, it too seemed upset at the
disturbance. With a few backward
glances in the vain hope of seeing the
kestrel again I headed for the car.

A vole, the kestrel's main diet

GOODBYE TO THE DAY

A teasel

Sitting relaxed near the bottom of a grassy slope, watching the sun go down on a summer evening, is a rare pleasure. I revelled in the unexpected opportunity. As the sun dropped closer to the horizon the sky turned from blue to deep yellow and then orangy red. Clouds turned a smoky purple, edged and streaked with rich deep crimson. Trees and plants became black velvet silhouettes against the reddening sky. The clear liquid warbling of a thrush filled the air with a melodious farewell to the day. Clouds of gnats danced in the air above me and flocks of starlings wheeled and circled towards their favourite roosting spots. The last rays of the sun burst through the clouds, like massive beams of searchlights. It was a spectacular end to the day that disappeared in seconds as the sun slipped below the earth's rim.

Bats were already beginning their nightly search for food as I walked past the small lake towards my car. Anglers discussed the day's catches as they packed away their

Beech trees at sunset in Shipley Country Park

equipment and ducks quacked a noisy goodnight to each other from the reeds. A pale light lingered on the horizon, but with the sun at last out of sight, shadows converged into a deep twilight. The first stars were shimmering in the sky as I reached home.

Sunset - a meadow brown butterfly becomes a black velvet silhouette against the reddening sky

HILLS AND VALLEYS

It had been a year or two since I had had the chance to wander along the valley of the river Dove. Thick grey clouds had brought heavy downpours over the previous few days but now those clouds were becoming thin, pale and ragged. At intervals the sun burst through with the promise of a warm bright day. I decided to begin my walk at Milldale and I'd soon crossed the Viator Bridge. The hills, rising up on both sides stretch one after another into the distance. Many of the hills are tree covered, softening and hiding their true shape, others look harsh and forbidding with jagged grey stones pushing their way through the soft summer green. A short springy turf, grazed by sheep, grows on the open slopes many of which are intersected by dry-stone walls and narrow rough tracks. I saw one of these walls climbing straight up to the brow of the hill, disappearing down the other side. Had there been a dispute in days past as to the ownership of the hill and this was how it had been resolved? Despite the formidable size and closeness of these hills there is no feeling of claustrophobia. In fact I'd almost forgotten the feeling of endless space and freedom these hills give you. Unlike the moors that have an aloof remoteness about them, the countryside around Dovedale has a familiar welcoming atmosphere to it.

Ignoring the hill paths I kept to the one by the river. It bubbled and sang over its stony bed. In many places the clear water is only inches deep with large rocks breaking the surface. A pair of grey wagtails were using them as platforms, flying from one to another as they searched for food. As the river took one of its many bends a dark brown bird, slightly larger than a sparrow flew swiftly past me downstream. Its flight was straight and low over the water. There was a flash of snow-white breast as it alighted on a half-submerged boulder and I realised it was a dipper. Slowly I made my way towards where it had landed and,

Milldale, a favourite haunt of the strikingly marked dipper

drawing level, I sat on the grassy river bank to watch the dipper as it began to feed. Here the river was shallow and fast flowing with little eddies swirling round the rocks and boulders. Clinging to the slippery rocks with long toes and strong claws the little bird plunged its head into the water again and again to feed on the insect larvae and other invertebrates that live there. While I sat watching, the dipper was joined by another. Both ignored me, intent on having a good breakfast. After about fifteen minutes I stood up intending to continue my walk but the dipper had another trick up his sleeve as I was about to find out. Up to this time both birds had been paddling around or climbing on the rocks in their search for food. Now one of them was wading towards deeper water. I

A buzzard

expected it to fly to the safety of a rock. But no, without further ado, the dipper tucked up his feet and floated on the water for a few feet. Then to my total amazement it suddenly dived beneath the surface and swam for two or three yards across the current to another group of rocks, where the water grew shallower again and the dipper surfaced and half-flew, half-hopped onto the nearest of them. With a quick shake and a cursory preen of the wings it began bobbing up and down. It could almost have been curtseying to an invisible audience pleased with its own cleverness. Though dippers look the sort of birds that belong in the treetops and fields, they are quite clearly as much at home in and under the water as the ducks with which they share the river. The river continued to take many twists and turns, the path following close by its side. Ravens Tor loomed higher and larger as I got nearer. Its exposed grey-white rock gleamed in the sunlight. Where the river passed below it, I stood still for a moment just staring up at it before carrying on through the now steep-sided gorge.

Buzzards have often been spotted flying and circling over the grass-topped hills and my eyes strayed repeatedly to the sky, hoping to catch sight of one. It was the black silhouettes of rooks and crows that dominated the lofty heights.

It's rare that you can be in the right place at the right time, or looking in the right direction when hoping for one of these remarkable sightings. This time luck was on my side. It was a buzzard I saw, but not soaring in the clear blue sky, this dark brown bird of prey flew out from the shelter of some trees on my left, and landed on top of a dry stone wall, a hundred yards ahead of me. It stared intently at the ground around its feet. As each step brought me closer to it, I expected the buzzard to take flight. It seemed to wait until the last second before spreading broad wings and moving to the new safer vantage point of a tree stump. Again, it scanned the ground looking for any movement that might be prey in the grass. The buzzard looked majestic, eagle-like as it perched there.

Ravens Tor

It didn't stay long on the tree stump. Though I stood still and watched at a discreet distance, the buzzard launched itself into the air and with a few steady wing beats, rose higher and higher and disappeared over the hills. I continued my walk, amazed once again at nature's rich diversity of wildlife.

41

A DELIGHT TO THE SENSES

The main path at Hilton Nature Reserve passes beside a large flower meadow. The assortment of flowers and variety of butterflies turned it into a carpet of living colour. One area near to the trees was dominated by pale pink flowers. I went for a closer look and discovered these clusters of tiny blooms were orchids. I later found out they were common spotted orchids. The path continued on through the trees to the lake. The shade under the trees gave a welcome respite from the glaring sun. A pair of moorhens scuttled across the trail in front of me and hid themselves in the thick reeds that bordered the water. Lingering under the cool overhanging branches I watched a family of Canada geese paddling their way to the bank to browse on the grass. As I walked on into the sunshine I was intrigued by the high number of damsel-flies that were hovering and weaving among the tall reeds. The pale greens, browns and flashy electric blue bodies were barely the size of matchsticks. Gossamer wings shimmered intangibly in the sunlight. Males were vying with each other for the females. Indeed some were already joined in the strange head to tail arrangement that damsel and dragonflies adopt during mating. Occasionally a much larger variety of damsel-fly flew in among them though they didn't stay long. At first their bodies looked black and there were large black spots on the wings, but as they caught the sunlight a rich deep blue-green sheen was revealed. These were banded agrions, more often seen near slow-flowing rivers and streams. The sun disappeared behind a stray cloud and the damsel-flies seemed to vanish into the foliage, they were difficult to see unless they moved. Following the various paths through wood, meadow and waterside I took in all the sights, sounds and smells. The day had been a veritable feast on the senses.

A banded agrion

*A meadow of buttercups and
pink-coloured common spotted orchids*

*inset: damsel-flies mating
left: a small tortoiseshell butterfly*

Curbar Edge looking
towards Calver

A huge rock formation
on Curbar Edge

MOORLAND MEETING

It was the middle of the night when I set out and I'd got an hour or so of driving ahead of me. Despite a midsummer heatwave the night air was quite chilly. As I drove the last few miles through the Chatsworth estate the sky grew lighter and I became aware of a grey mist covering the moors ahead of me, just where I happened to be making for. Walking the last mile across the moor, I headed for a small reservoir fed by a brook that wound its way through a narrow channel with sloping sides. It was only a fortnight before, I'd discovered that a small colony of adders lived here on a south-facing bank well above the water. During the hottest part of summer, adders are more likely to bask in the early morning or late afternoon when the temperature isn't so high. Hence my pre-dawn journey. Finding a suitable spot to sit and observe them before they emerged to catch the warmth of the sun meant I wouldn't disturb them later. This summer had been exceptionally hot and dry so I was sure they would be out soon after sunrise. I hadn't reckoned with the thick mist that was being blown at some speed across the wide expanse of moorland. No snakes would be out for a while yet, all I could do was sit and wait. A flat-topped rock made a convenient seat, but the small scrubby bushes that were dotted here and there on the bank offered no protection from the biting wind.

With neither trees nor buildings to break up the scene, the undulating landscape seemed to go on and on for ever. Yet less than two miles west of where I sat, the moor ended abruptly at Curbar Edge and Froggatt Edge. There is a breathtaking bird's-eye view over the river Derwent and the nearby villages of Curbar, Froggatt and Calver. The grass in the main is of a coarse wiry sort, well suited to surviving in this bleak countryside. Heather grows profusely, mingled here and there with large clumps of bracken giving a pleasing mottled effect to the landscape. Huge grey rocks loomed up randomly out of the vegetation. Looking at them I could almost believe some giant out of a mythical past had stood throwing them as part of a great game. Sheep graze the moor, wandering about in small groups, their gurgling bleats had an eerie sound through the mist.

An hour passed as I sat and looked around me. The sun was gaining strength, the

A typical Derbyshire moorland scene

A female adder displays her beautifully ornate markings

hazy-looking globe shone intermittently through the slowly thinning mist. Now was the time to select a good spot and wait, hopefully, for the adders to appear. I wasn't sure what to expect. The only other time I'd seen a live adder in the 'wild' it looked in a sorry state. I was about fourteen, living on the outskirts of Leicester close to a large deer park that I visited regularly. A foolish youngster had somehow managed to capture one in a big glass jar and then didn't know what to do with it. The adder looked drab and distressed, continuously attacking the sides of the jar in an attempt to escape. It was eventually handed over to a park ranger to be released in a suitably quiet place. While musing over my previous encounter with an adder, I walked warily to a grassy area at one side of the bank. The grass quickly gave way to an expanse of heather. At the edge of the heather, half hidden, was a low flat stone. A perfect basking place, or so I hoped. I was given no time to prepare myself. A sudden movement, sensed rather than seen, out of the corner of my eye made me turn swiftly, just in time to see a large female adder glide quickly into the thick tangle of grass a yard or two to my left. An instant later a smaller, much darker one, disappeared into the undergrowth almost at my feet. I was stunned by the richness of the colours, made more intense by the distinctive zigzag pattern. Cautiously, taking a few more steps towards the flat stone, I scanned the ground carefully. I became aware of movement in the heather that was growing around it. Slowly dropping to my knees, I edged forward for a closer look. Coming to a halt a discreet two feet away I peered into the heather. Entwined amidst its branches lay not one but two of these beautiful reptiles. They didn't seem to be aware of me yet, so I took the opportunity to study them in more detail. Both were female of about the same size, making it difficult to differentiate between the two bodies. At this proximity I noticed the pale biscuit colour had a faint greenish hue and the dark chocolate pattern that was edged with black, also had a greenish hue when the sunlight fell on it.

The mist had completely disappeared by now and I could feel the heat of the sun on my back. The adders must have felt the rise in temperature too and I watched as their lithe bodies slithered apart. One moved out of the heather to the grass at the other end of the rock to me. Instead of curling up again it stretched out in a series of curves, flattening its body to gain maximum exposure. The other snake was about to follow suit when it became aware of me. It made no attempt to go under cover. The red eye with its black slit of a pupil stared directly at me, waiting to see what I would do. I moved my hand an inch

White Edge moor

or two towards it, creating a shadow over its head and part of its body. In a slow deliberate fashion the adder eased itself back deeper into the heather, head raised, still eyeing me warily. At the same time it started to flick its tongue in and out, tasting the air to find out more about this intrusion of its territory. Curious to see the adder's reaction, I moved back to my original position. After a few minutes the snake seemed to sense the immediate danger had passed and appeared to relax. Gradually it brought its supple curves further out into the sun. I moved towards the adder again, the effect was a repeat of the first time, except now it gave a faint warning hiss. A definite, keep out of my space noise. I backed off, not in fear of getting bitten, but respectful of the fact that I was the intruder.

An emperor moth caterpillar

So preoccupied had I been with this snake I hadn't noticed that another had joined the one in the grass to my right. Smaller and much darker, it made a spectacular display of colour in the bright sunlight. Increasing heat brought about a changing of positions from the snakes. I watched as they lazily slid back into the dappled shading of the heather. Here they would be protected from the direct rays of the sun. The time was fast approaching mid-morning and I knew the adders would soon return to their underground burrows to avoid the midday heat. It was time to leave them in peace. Slowly I got to my feet, the snakes continued to bask unperturbed. It occurred to me on looking down into the grass and heather, that even from this short distance, the adders were difficult to discern amongst the vegetation. For such ornate creatures this didn't seem possible. Stepping carefully through the undergrowth I made my way back to the path. The sun now blazed fiercely in a cloudless blue sky. Even the sheep had stopped grazing to find shady spots under tall bracken leaves or beneath the overhang of the larger boulders. The midday heat made the walk back to the car seem much longer. The day had become lazy. I decided to sit for a while on one of the large rocks that pushed out of the heather at the side of the path. A few bees were buzzing nearby, searching out the pinky purple flowers that were just beginning to open. There was a tiny splash of brighter colour in a clump of heather on my right. It was a large plump caterpillar that was feeding on the leaves. As brilliant as a neon sign it was coloured bright green with thin black bands down the length of its body. It was the larva of an emperor moth munching its way tirelessly through the heather leaves. If it survived being eaten itself, the caterpillar would spend the winter hidden away among the heather in a cocoon and emerge as an adult moth next spring. Driving home through the dusty towns full of noisy traffic and people, the quiet emptiness of the moor seemed a million miles away. I looked forward to many more enjoyable visits in the future.

ON YOUR DOORSTEP

As a child, I knew gardens were attractive to wild creatures, but at first thought, only for birds and insects. Putting food out daily, I watched from a window to see which birds came to feed. In spring and summer, armed with a field guide, I would try to put names to the various butterflies, moths and 'creepy crawlies' that frequented the flowers and vegetables. Over the years, I discovered that there is a much greater diversity of wildlife in our gardens. It is not usual now for family, friends and acquaintances to tell me of visitors or inhabitants to be seen. It might be hedgehogs snorting and snuffling on their nightly search for food, frogs taking up residence in a garden pond or a wood mouse finding a warm safe haven in someone's garden shed. So when a voice on the telephone asked me if I wanted to see wild foxes at close quarters, I readily accepted. Visions of a hidden copse somewhere near Spondon were quickly replaced with wonder when he told me a vixen, occasionally accompanied by a dog fox, regularly visited his and neighbours' gardens to feed on scraps put out for them. Early evening a couple of days later found me sitting with the gentleman on his patio not knowing what to expect and asking numerous questions. Suddenly a red shape was spotted through the hedge trotting purposefully along the road towards the garden.

I held my breath as with cat-like agility the female fox picked her way among the flowers towards us. Three or four yards away she stopped, suddenly aware of me, a stranger in *her* garden. For seconds, yellow eyes stared at me and then, with an air of aloofness, I was disregarded in favour of the food offered by the houseowner. She gently took the food in her mouth but didn't eat it. Instead the gleaming chestnut-coloured vixen disappeared back through the hedge. I guessed she was taking it to a hidden lair where cubs were being raised. Returning after a second trip back to the den, I ventured to offer some of the food myself. To my lasting delight, she cautiously sniffed my hand with outstretched pointed nose. Her breath felt warm on my fingers. She refused to take the food but I wasn't surprised or disappointed at this. It had taken the man many months to gain the trust of this beautiful wild creature. The fox's guarded acceptance of me was only because she felt safe on his

The wood mouse makes a home in a garden shed

49

property. How different this reaction was to a fox living in another part of Derbyshire. This one refused to have any close contact with humans even though it came nightly to one garden where food was put out for it. Though a member of the dog family, foxes are very cat-like in their behaviour. And just like a cat, I was told, this fox I'd met could be friendly one minute then ignore you the next. It saddens me that foxes are invariably spoken about in a derogatory fashion. Words like cunning, sly and crafty are all used in a negative way. Yet the fox, like most wild animals, has to rely on instinct and resourcefulness and have the skill in using them to survive. I for one admire their ingenuity. As darkness fell I made my way home with the thought running through my head that our encounters with the wildlife around us can begin from the moment we step out of our doors.

Above: A great tit

Left: Blue and willow tits are regular visitors to garden food dispensers

Below: An adult blue tit lands on a peanut feeder

A hedgehog

*The Nuthatch searches
for food in the garden*

The cunning fox

51

AERIAL ACROBATS

Mid to late summer brings about a lull in nature's activities. After spring's frantic bustle of growing, producing flowers, courtship, mating and rearing families, everything seems to relax and take a breather. Leaves were missing their earlier brilliance, they had a dull lacklustre appearance. Even the flowers had lost their former sparkle, petals were lost and many had a drab, dingy look about them. The tall red spikes of the willow-herbs were now beginning to seed. A gentle breeze lifted the fluffy, lighter-than-air, seed-bearers and carried them far across the countryside. They drifted and floated through the air like snowflakes in winter. Blackberries cried out from their thorny stems to be eaten. Lingering a while I savoured the sweet, dark, juicy fruits. There seemed to be fewer butterflies about now, except for the odd small copper and common blue. They didn't stay settled for long. Their colours flashed in the sun as they flitted from plant to plant, staying close to the ground. I made my way towards a line of shrubby trees that bordered a winding brook feeding Oakerthorpe's pond. Hidden by the thick tangle of undergrowth and wide branching bushes was, hopefully, a narrow path leading to a small rarely used bridge over the brook. After crossing and emerging from the grasping foliage, the air was warm and still, sheltered from the breeze by tall, dense, hawthorn bushes. Dragonflies become active in late summer and I was hoping to catch sight of some of the larger species over nearby reed beds. I was surprised by the number of peacock butterflies that haunted this small area. Ignoring the more colourful flowers, they competed for space on the dull, pinkish-green flowers of the dwarf elder. As they rested on the flower heads, they lazily opened and closed their wings, displaying the brilliantly coloured eye spots. Having the opportunity to admire these beautiful insects at such close quarters made me forget for a while my intended search for dragonflies. Butterflies appear so delicate and ephemeral that it may come as a surprise to realise that many, like the peacock, actually hibernate through the winter. The world about me became bathed in silence. It was a peaceful summer silence. Though birds gave an occasional whistle and bees buzzed from flower to flower, the sounds seemed muffled by a wall of heat, so engrossed was I in the activities of the butterflies.

While leaning over the bushes I sensed some sort of activity taking place above me. Turning to look up, my first reaction was to duck and cover my head. What seemed like hundreds of large dragonflies darted and wheeled just a foot or so above my head. It was like a scene from the Battle of Britain. So close were they I could hear the faint clip of wings as they narrowly missed colliding into each other while passing to and fro in the air above me. I watched fascinated. Their high speed flight took them past trees and bushes and quickly out of sight. A few stragglers continued to skim over

A common blue butterfly

A bee approaches a rosebay willow-herb

Opposite: a dragonfly emerges from its nymph state to become adult

53

the greenery around me hoping to catch any remaining prey. It was at this point that I discovered how they catch their food. Hoverflies were abundant and wasps, looking deliciously evil in their black and yellow jackets, were enjoying the sweet juices of summer berries. One such wasp having taken its fill from a nearby bramble lazily rose into the air. With the accuracy and speed of a swooping falcon one of the large brown and blue dragonflies scooped up the wasp in legs that it used like a net. The powerful jaws were already devouring the wasp as it settled on a branch to finish its meal. After eating, the dragonfly rested for a while. The whole of its body started to vibrate rapidly. I gently touched the twig it was resting on, I could feel the reverberation through my fingers. As the vibration went through its wings they gave off a faint hum. It was as if it was revving up its engine ready for flight. And, as if on cue, seconds later the dragonfly launched itself into the air to begin hunting again. By this time the large mass of dragonflies was working its way back towards me. It made me think of the swarms of locusts I'd seen on television. I reached up with my hands. There were so many of them I could feel their wings brush past my fingers.

The beautifully marked and appropriately named peacock butterfly

I spent an enthralling hour or two watching the antics of the dragonflies and butterflies, but as the afternoon wore on they gradually decreased in number until only an odd one here and there remained. Filled with a mood of quiet contentment I made my way slowly back home.

A four-spotted chaser dragonfly

Autumn leaves - a beech

A chestnut

55

CAUGHT IN THE CROSSFIRE

With nothing more than a sniff of the air you can tell when autumn has arrived. That sharpness that clears the head and makes your nose tingle inside. Trees have already begun their colour transformation. Pale yellows and golds stand out amidst the muted green canopy of leaves. Some like the maple and beech are already turning a deep russet. I'd left the hustle and bustle of Derby behind and was heading for Chaddesden Wood.

By mid-morning I was clambering through the undergrowth of this mature, mainly deciduous wood. A dawn mist, though itself gone, had left everywhere damp and dripping. Fine beads of moisture clung to the cobwebs. They covered the bracken like tattered net curtains. It's only on days like this, when the cobwebs are bathed in dew, that you realise just how many spiders there must be around us. A couple of grey squirrels were chasing each other around the trees. They raced at breakneck speed, jumping from branch to branch, circling the trees. Then, careering headlong down the trunks, they'd bounce along the grass to the next tree. One of the squirrels waited in ambush for the other. Clinging somewhat precariously to the side of a tree, he peered round cautiously. With tail flicking up and down in excitement he made a sudden dash, bowling the other one over. After a quick scuffle they separated and faced each other for a second or two, then, with a twisting leap into the air, the game of tag started again. The mixed smell of leaf-mould, rotting wood and wet vegetation filled me with a sense, not of death and decay, as one might expect, but of growth and continuation. Autumn is the time of year when fungus is at its most prolific and woods like these, with plenty of undergrowth and rotting dead wood, seem ideal. Fungi come in

The distinctive fly agaric toadstool

many shapes and sizes. The typical umbrella shaped toadstool is the most frequently seen. But there are others that resemble branching corals or small footballs. I was surprised by the range of colours to be found. Brilliant yellows, deep reds, snowy whites and glowing oranges. The most eyecatching I've seen must be the fly agaric. The vivid red cap, spotted with white, rivals the more conventional flowers for showiness. I decided many years ago not to touch or remove fungi of any sort. Many are poisonous.

Distinguishing these from similar looking edible and non-poisonous ones is not a task I'm qualified to perform. My solution is to treat all fungi as potentially poisonous and buy my mushrooms at the supermarket. As I walked between the trees peering under bracken and bramble for the more elusive specimens, I realised I could have been missing many more unusual ones that were out in the open. Though the majority of fungi grow at ground level on fallen trees and among decaying vegetation, many take up residence on living trees high on the trunks.

The light fresh breeze that had gently rippled the grass and sent leaves swirling to the ground, suddenly increased in strength. Branches above me started to sway to and fro, sounding like distant gunshots as they crashed together. Leaves that had fallen to the ground twisted and twirled back into the air to meet those coming off the trees. Drops of rain, cold and stinging, plunged through the thinning canopy. A nearby oak tree looked as if it would afford some shelter as it still had most of its leaves. I leant against the rough bark and stared up towards the darkening sky. Moments later a more violent gust of wind brought down a hail of acorns, followed almost immediately by a second bombardment from a different direction. Feeling as if I was in the middle of a war zone, I decided discretion would definitely be the better part of valour, so facing the rain, I made my way back along the track towards my car. The downpour was short-lived and the heavy grey clouds were soon moving away, revealing a sapphire blue sky overhead. Flashing and bouncing off every leaf and twig, the sun brought colour and life back to the wood. The wind remained strong with gusts, first from one direction then another, making even the thickest branches toss about like corn in a field. The noise filled my head with a vision of rocky seashore cliffs and huge white topped breakers crashing over them. I was brought out of my reverie by a loud crack close behind me. A large branch, now swinging like a pendulum had snapped almost clean through on a tree only ten yards away.

Twigs, leaves and other debris flew in all directions. The wind buffeted me from all sides. At times it was hard to take a step or catch my breath. I finally emerged from the trees and climbed the stile into the country lane. Luckily my car was parked nearby and I quickly got into its calm refuge. The wind screeched and whistled mercilessly across the open fields as I drove carefully home. Not all days are good for walking and exploring and some can be positively dangerous, but that day in the wood would certainly stick in my memory.

Left: a grey squirrel
Right: a silver birch plays host to
'birch polypore' sometimes called razor-strop fungus

ICY ESCAPADES

Cold winds and stinging rain, dark mornings that fail miserably to brighten up as the day progresses, mists and fogs, grey, cheerless and depressing. Underfoot, everything is squelchy and muddy. Everywhere looks dirty and feels dirty. Rarely do you see any animals, and birds too seem loath to venture far from the sanctuary of hedgerows and trees. Their half-hearted whistles and chirps add to the feeling of melancholy.

Though it's still good to get out in the open and get some 'fresh' air, the bleak climate seems to drain away any enthusiasm that was felt when starting out. Even the most stalwart of ramblers, who goes out in all weathers, must find inspiration to be at a low ebb. Yes, you've guessed, this is a typical winter's day in Derbyshire. But here and there among the gloomy days there are times when, with a change in the weather, the countryside almost drags you from your house, it's so inviting. I woke up on one such morning to find bright cold sunlight shining through the windows, enticing me out into the lanes and fields. Clothed warmly against the cold, I was soon out walking. A heavy overnight frost and a light covering of snow had cloaked the landscape in a crisp spiky mantle that gleamed with icing-sugar whiteness. A nearby lake was frozen over two-thirds of its surface. Only the tireless labour of a group of swans, paddling sedately up and down, kept a small area free of ice. Ducks, mostly mallards, coots and gulls waddled slowly and uncertainly over the slippery veneer. Others stood in little groups, all facing the same way, letting the momentary warmth of the weak winter sun wash over their backs. With a rowdy fanfare of quacks, a half-dozen or so ducks flew over the trees and with a final sweeping curve landed on the ice. Unable to get a grip on the slippery surface, a reaction, almost of panic, spread through them. Webbed

*A coot studies
itself in the ice*

'The clear blue of the sky created a sharp contrast.'

feet began to back-pedal furiously trying to gain a purchase on the ice. At the same time wings were flapping vigorously to help brake their speed and keep them upright. As alarm spread to the other birds the whole lake reverberated with their startled cries. Gulls simultaneously launched themselves into the air screeching their displeasure at the disruption. The ducks didn't take flight, instead they ran, or rather waddled, with wings outstretched for balance, across the icy lake. They looked like unskilled tight-rope walkers practising their high wire act. It took some minutes for the commotion to settle down, only the swans seemed unperturbed by the incident.

Turning for a last look across the lake before carrying on I faced into the keen wind. Showers of frost were blown from nearby trees, the small ice crystals hitting my face felt refreshing and tingly. Low in the sky the sun's light was reflected white and sparkling off every plant, twig and blade of grass. The clear blue of the sky created a sharp contrast, that intensified the frost's whiteness. It was only on closer examination of the dried skeleton of a nearby plant that I was able to appreciate the ornate delicacy of this natural phenomenon that is all too easily overlooked. The heavy frost had built up over the hours of darkness and each of the many pointed miniature icicles had grown to nearly a centimetre long. Covering leaf and stalk these tiny spines stuck out in all directions looking like a frozen cactus in a desert of ice and snow.

My walk took me to a narrow fast-moving stream. Unaffected by the freezing weather it rattled and bubbled on its way, passing under the concrete and iron bridge on which I was now standing. Leaning on the railing I stared into the dark, cold-looking water as it splashed and gurgled towards me. There were still a few red berries on the bushes that grew on the steep banks, dangling their black and bony finger-like branches into the water. Small movements in one of these bushes, growing a yard or two from the bridge, caught my eye. I thought they were birds, maybe sparrows or finches, that were after the berries, but no, the small brown creatures moving along the branches were water voles. They're often mistaken for and called water rats. But if you look carefully, their ears and eyes are smaller and they have a much rounder more appealing appearance. I counted about half-a-dozen of them scampering from a hidden hole in the bank to the bunches of crimson fruit and back again. They were great acrobats, running and balancing with ease on the thin twigs. Sometimes the voles would pick up the berries and eat them immediately, but mostly they collected them in their mouths and took them back to the burrow. Even when two met head-on along a narrow branch they weren't flustered. One would stop and the other would crawl over its body and back onto the branch. Both then continued on their way. Minutes passed as I watched fascinated by their apparent teamwork. It was at a much later date that I found out that it is only in winter that they get together like this. Most of the year they are solitary, very territorial animals.

Engrossed in the antics of the water voles it was a while before I noticed other sights and sounds around me. It was the clear piping whistle of a robin that attracted me first, but as I listened and looked around, I realised a whole variety of birds was bustling about, revelling in the brief but welcome sunshine. Leaving the bridge I walked towards an assortment of bushes that flanked the footpath. The robin was perched on a low branch watching over his smalll kingdom. He fluffed his feathers and shook his wings, looking first one way, and then the other, alert to any intruders. As he hopped from branch to ground and back again he was quite unconcerned about the sparrows, blackbirds etc. that settled near him. But when suddenly another robin alighted on a neighbouring branch he went into action. Claws splayed forward, he dived at the invader. For a few seconds they fought literally tooth and claw. Wings flapping, beaks stabbing and pecking, they grappled like two prize fighting cocks. Just as suddenly it was over, the intruder was defeated and sent on his way. Triumphantly, the robin flew back to his look-out post on the bush and gave a quick whistle of victory, then with feathers fluffed up against the cold he began to forage for food.

Taking the left-hand fork of the pathway I walked slowly, the frozen grass crunching beneath my feet. After a few yards I turned and looked back. I felt an almost childlike pleasure inside me when I saw that mine were the only footprints on the snowy white carpet. Though the path is used frequently by many people, at that moment I was a lone explorer leaving my mark on an uninhabited island.

'The robin was perched on a low branch watching over his small kingdom'

REBIRTH

Gone are the frozen lakes and ponds, and the sugar coating of overnight frosts. Icicles that hung like glass stalactites from the rocks of cascading rivers and streams have melted and dripped away. The winter we are left with is grey and cheerless. A dull, cold, misty morning shows little change through the day. As January drifts unnoticeably into February, I start to get the feeling that winter is going on forever. On each walk in the countryside there appears no sign of renewed life. Spring seems reluctant to show her face.

Imperceptibly at first, the days get longer and the temperature rises. Birdsong changes and becomes more insistent as territory is contested with greater fervour. The search is on to find a mate and raise a family. To be woken by the 'dawn chorus' always fills me with hope for the day. Catkins appear almost overnight. One minute there are no signs on branch or twig, then suddenly the yellow 'tails' are quivering in the breeze. A week or two later the furry, silver pussy willow 'paws' shimmer from the hedgerows. Now I know spring is almost here and I get a sense of impatient excitement inside me, confident that new life is bubbling to get under way. It's the time to rediscover the familiar places and explore as if for the first time all that the countryside has to offer.

'A week or two later the furry, silver pussy willow 'paws' shimmer from the hedgerows'

'Confident new life is bubbling to get under way'

Jean Woolley

Living in Ilkeston most of her life, Jean Woolley grew up discovering that Derbyshire was both varied and interesting to someone with a keen sense of observation. From an early age she took an avid and enquiring interest in the wildlife around her area. With English and Art being her favourite subjects at school, it wasn't long before Jean was writing descriptive, individual and personal essays, on what was, and still is, a love and appreciation of the countryside and its inhabitants. These experiences led to weekly newspaper columns and magazine articles. This book is a natural progression from her earlier work.

Stuart Whitehead

After living in Nottingham, Leicester and Lincolnshire, Stuart Whitehead came to Derby in 1975 and now regards Derbyshire as his home county. As a freelance photographer, Stuart has worked for most of our local newspapers, and has had work published in the national press, magazines and on postcards. Having covered Royal visits, sports events and public relations assignments, Stuart considers wildlife photography the most challenging and rewarding. The photographs in this book were all taken in Derbyshire over a five year period.